A BEGINNER'S GUIDE TO DIVIDEND STOCK INVESTING

JAMES PATTERSENN JR.

www.theintelligentinvestorhub.com

www.howtoinvestinstocks.org

CONTENTS

DISCLAIMER

This book was published for educational purposes, and it's not intended to provide specific personalized advice. It's sold with the understanding that the author or publisher is not engaged in rendering legal, accounting, investment or other professional services. Investing in stocks and the stock market involves varying degrees of risk, and there's no assurance that a specific stock, investment principle or investment strategy will be profitable for an individual, group or organization. All information contained in this book was gathered from sources believed to be reliable, but neither the author nor the publisher can accept responsibility for its accuracy.

The author or publisher specifically denies any responsibility for liability, loss, or risk, professional or otherwise, which is incurred as a consequence, directly or indirectly, of the use and application of any of the contents of this book.

ISBN 978-0-9895464-9-2 (Softcover)
ISBN 978-1-7365803-0-1 (eBook)

YOUR FREE GIFT

Thanks for purchasing my book!

As a way of showing my appreciation, I want to send you my FREE REPORT.

5 STOCKS THAT WARREN BUFFETT WOULD LOVE

Contained within this report are:

- 5 wonderful companies that Warren Buffett might buy today if given the opportunity.
- The specific criteria for picking Buffett type stocks via value investing.
- Great companies that are practically guaranteed to grow and deliver big returns well beyond the pandemic!

Enter your email at the link below and I will send you a copy of this Free Report:

https://mailchi.mp/b65776af6219/5-stocks-warren-buffett-would-love

1

DIVIDEND STOCK INVESTING: WHAT IS IT?

Dividend stock investing, which I will often just refer to as dividend investing throughout this book, is an investment strategy in which an investor invests in stocks or other equities that pay dividends in order to generate a dependable and stable stream of income from said stocks or equities. Dividend investing is a great strategy for individuals from all walks of life who want to build wealth and achieve financial freedom. It can be a very rewarding approach for investors looking to generate income or build wealth by reinvesting dividends received. In addition, dividend investors can expect to see appreciations in the price of their stocks; and this appreciation is known as capital gains or capital appreciation.

Dividends are the payments that the company makes to its shareholders out of its earnings. The company's Board of Directors authorizes dividend payments and the total amount of dividends distributed (paid out) is established by the board as well.

Historically, dividend investing has offered higher returns and has been less volatile than the S&P 500 Index. The S&P 500 Index is a market-capitalization weighted index of the 500 largest publicly-traded companies here in the United States. So we are talking about some very large and financially sound companies. The S&P 500 index is also used as a yardstick by many financial institutions to compare their investment performance to that of the overall stock market.

According to an October 2019 Kiplinger article, the Dividend Aristocrats Index returned an annual average of 18.3% over the previous 10 year period researched, compared with 17.1% (including dividends) for the S&P 500 as a whole, and did so with less volatility than the S&P 500 Index. Even a large percentage of the S&P 500 Index returns are the result of reinvested dividends. According to research performed by the Hartford Funds, 78% of the total returns achieved by the S&P 500 Index can be attributed to reinvested dividends.

On average, an investor that builds a solid portfolio of dividend stocks can expect the income created through the portfolio to grow 5 to 10% annually with dividends reinvested. In addition to receiving dividends, investors can also expect appreciation in the value of their stocks. Those that might consider using dividend investing are investors desiring a steady stream of income that increases annually, investors wanting an approach to investing that's almost passive once the portfolio is established, and investors of all ages wanting to build wealth and achieve financial freedom over the long-term using a proven strategy that works.

2

GETTING STARTED WITH DIVIDEND STOCKS

The very first thing to do to get started is open an online investment account such as an Individual Retirement Account (IRA) if you don't already have one. The online account allows you to place all of your trades from the comfort of your home and allows you to easily monitor your portfolio. In addition, you receive special benefits such as deferred taxes for investing through a retirement account. There's usually a minimum deposit required to open any sort of investment account regardless of the type with one exception: the Individual Retirement Account with direct rollovers from other retirement accounts are usually permitted with no minimum and are free-of-charge. The minimum deposit varies with each financial institution and with the type of account being established. It will be necessary for you to research several brokerages to find the one that's right for you. If necessary, consult with a financial professional for help establishing your investment or retirement account.

Once the account has been established, set up direct deposit through your employer if it's available. Direct deposit allows you to have a percentage of your pay or a dollar amount of your pay that you specify deposited into your brokerage account automatically. The use of direct deposit makes saving easy; with its use, you are actually paying yourself first. The failure of most people to pay themselves first is the main reason many of them find themselves living from paycheck to paycheck, even after many years of working.

If you are self-employed or your company does not offer direct deposit, there's still another way to make investing automatic and it's through the use of automatic transfers. Automatic transfers are transfers that your bank will make for you by taking money from an account that you designate and depositing it into another account. Automatic transfers are an excellent way to go if direct deposit is not available for you. The transactions are performed online and can be completed within a matter of seconds with today's computers.

Next, if you are just starting, I recommend that you set a goal to deposit a minimum of $50 per week or $100 biweekly into your brokerage account. Doing so will give you $200-$250 to invest each month. In a year's time, you could actually save as much as $2600. With it, you could easily buy several dividend stocks for your portfolio. Of course if you can save more, do it.

I have been investing for many years now and place all of my trades online and have never had any problems. I do recommend that you choose a reputable online broker such as TD Ameritrade®, E*Trade®, or Charles Schwab®. Every time the cash balance in my brokerage account hit the $500 mark, I would purchase shares of stock for my account. Using the method described, within a few years my brokerage account went from the original deposit of around

$500 to more than $30,000. Although $30,000 might not sound like much for some, at the time I had been living paycheck to paycheck and thought that it was impossible for me to even save money, not to mention invest it.

You do not need to wait for your cash balance to reach $500 before buying shares. When I started investing, I paid a commission with each purchase. Most brokerages no longer charge a commission to purchase most types of securities. Even when selling, fees are almost non-existent today. If you build your portfolio in the manner described, I believe that you will find yourself with an impressive portfolio in a very short period of time.

3

TWELVE PRINCIPLES FOR INVESTING LIKE A PRO

There are some simple, yet powerful principles that can help you succeed in stock market investing. A lot of research went into determining the twelve principles revealed here. When studying and researching some of the world's most successful investors, I discovered that these twelve principles tended to be universal among them, which means that these time-tested principles are very important for long-term investment success. Although the principles may appear to be simple or common sense, the majority of those that invest in the stock market fail to use them. I believe those investors that are willing to adhere to these principles will be very happy with the long-term performance of their portfolios.

Principle #1: Stick with the stocks of businesses that you understand.

If you don't understand a business, don't purchase its stock. Investors are more likely to pick better-performing stocks if they purchase the stocks of businesses that they understand. Usually those easy-to-understand, boring businesses are the ones that make money year after year. It has been said many times that a good investment is usually a boring one.

Principle #2: Be a long-term investor.

Warren Buffett has said that if you don't plan on holding a stock for 10 years, you have no business holding it for 10 minutes. Holding a stock for the long-term is the most effective way to maximize your return since a stock's earnings will usually increase dramatically over time along with its book value. These increases will result in the stock trading at a significantly higher price over the long term and if the stock pays dividends, the dividends are likely to grow consistently also.

Principle #3 Try to purchase stocks when they are trading at low P/E ratios.

Look for stocks trading significantly below their average annual price-to-earnings ratio for the last seven to 10 years. The price-to-earnings ratio is normally referred to simply as the P/E ratio.

The equation that follows demonstrates how the P/E of a stock is determined:

$$\frac{\text{Price Per Share}}{\text{Earnings Per Share}} = \text{P/E Ratio}$$

For example, a stock is currently trading on the market for $40 per share. It has $2 in total estimated earnings for the year. The calculation would look like this:

$$\frac{\$40}{\$2} = 20 \text{ or a P/E of } 20$$

The P/E for the stock is 20. If this P/E is lower than the average annual P/E of the stock for the last seven to 10 years, then the stock is probably cheap based on what investors have been willing to pay for the shares in the past. Another important thing that you should know is not to avoid stocks just because they are trading at what appears to be high P/E ratios. History has shown us that many high P/E stocks that seemed to be too expensive have proven to be long-term winners. A good example of this kind of stock is Amazon.com, Inc.

Principle #4: Buy low and sell high.

Most investors tend to buy high and sell low, doing the exact opposite of what they should do. They buy an overvalued stock and when there's a market sell-off, they panic and sell too. This results in them selling the stock for much less than they paid for it. For intelligent investors, this market sell-off is a great time to buy excellent stocks at a discount.

Principle #5: Don't buy a stock just because it's cheap.

Everyone would love to be able to purchase a stock for $1 and watch it skyrocket to $40 before selling it, but that rarely happens. If a stock is very cheap or has recently lost most of its value, then something fundamental to the success of the business has other investors concerned. Look for undervalued, high-quality stocks instead of cheap stocks, and never buy a stock because it used to be $40 a share and now trades for $2 per share. If a stock's price has been on a continuous downhill slope and the stock has lost most of its value, think long and hard before purchasing it because there is probably something wrong concerning the business.

Principle #6: Select stocks that have strong brand appeal.

Look for businesses that have strong brand appeal when purchasing stocks. A strong brand appeal gives them a durable competitive advantage over their competition. Examples are Nike, PepsiCo, Wal-Mart, Under Armour, and Walgreens. Almost everyone has heard of these businesses or has purchased the products that they sell. When consumers see a brand name, they expect to receive high-quality products at a fair price.

Principle #7: Diversify your portfolio.

Diversification is one of the most important elements necessary for successful investing. When it comes to stocks, you should never put all of your eggs in one basket. Diversification reduces risk and improves an investor's opportunity for a better return. A diversified portfolio is one that consists of stocks from a variety of industries and sectors. For example, if you have decided to create a portfolio that will contain a total of five stocks, it would be unwise to hold five stocks from the same industry in that portfolio, such as five oil company stocks. The best and safest approach would be to purchase five stocks from five completely different industries. In doing so, if one or two of the industries suffer because of some economic turmoil, the other stocks should not be affected much.

Principle #8: Keep your emotions in check.

Never make an investment decision that is based just on your feelings or emotions. Think about a scientist. A scientist is always concerned about the facts or the evidence that is present. You must be a scientist in the investment world. Always get the facts before buying or selling a stock. Emotions are the cause of a lot of the stock market's volatility, but when the underlying factors are checked, most of the time nothing notable has changed in the stock market that warrants the volatility.

Principle #9: Watch out for greed.

Never allow greed to cause you to make very risky or foolish decisions when investing. It is the number one killer of an investor's wealth. It causes investors to make rash decisions without much thought or research. The smart investor is able to benefit from the greed of others.

Principle #10: Do your own homework.

This is a biggie when it comes to investing. Please do your own research before investing your hard-earned money into any investment. All too often investors are willing to put their money into recommendations from individuals that have less knowledge about investing than themselves. Always do your own research to learn everything that you can about an investment. I believe that you can do a much better job managing your portfolio and finances than many of the investment experts out there. Research has revealed that 90% of fund managers fail to outperform the market over the long-term. Unlike the investment adviser or fund manager that may have hundreds of accounts under management, you will only need to be concerned with your account and can therefore fully commit yourself to making the best choices and decisions concerning it.

Principle #11: Don't lose money.

This is exactly what's going to happen if you attempt to get-rich-quick or to time the stock market. When investing in stocks, you must be able to cope with your investments falling drastically in price without you panicking and selling your stocks at a loss. It's not uncommon for very good stocks to fall 50% or more in value in any given year, and that's definitely not something I enjoy seeing. If it happens to you, your response should be to hang in there if you know that you have made the right choice. Better yet, buy some more of the stock if its fundamentals have not changed or have improved. Most importantly, have the goal and the determination to not lose any of your money from investing.

Principle #12: Be a patient investor.

The world's most successful investors did not amass their fortunes overnight. It took some time to do so. Time and the power of compounding are an investor's greatest allies. Warren Buffett has said, "The stock market is a device for transferring money from the impatient to the patient." So, as you strive to build wealth and achieve financial freedom, be sure to practice patience.

4

COMPOUND GROWTH: MAKE MONEY WHILE YOU SLEEP!

Many years ago I remember hearing a report on television that told how much money basketball legend Michael Jordon was making while he slept. Of course, the large amount that was reported fascinated me at the time and I thought to myself how wonderful it would be if I could make money while I slept. Imagine going to bed at night and waking up the next morning with more money in your account than you had the night before. Wouldn't that be nice? In my mind, owning dividend stocks is about the closest most of us will come to that realization.

Although we won't receive daily payments, we can expect to receive quarterly payments at least four times yearly and if the company distributes dividends monthly, we can expect to receive payments from it twelve times a year. Now here's the great thing about dividend investing; your dividend stocks will be working for you 24 hours a day and 7 days a week as long as you own them, and they will continue to consistently spew money into your investment account regardless of whether you are asleep or awake.

Warren Buffett, the Sage of Omaha, stated "If you don't find a way to make money while you sleep, you will work until you die." To put it simply, Buffett was saying even when you're asleep; your money should be working for you. I think one of the best ways to let your money work for you even when you're sleep is through a combination of dividend reinvesting along with the power of compounding that result from those dividends. The reinvesting of all dividends that are earned from investing results in your money growing exponentially. This growth is known as compound growth. Compound growth is what allows an investor to take a small sum of money and in time become extremely wealthy. It has been called the "Eighth Wonder of the World." If a person had bought just 10 shares of Berkshire stock for a mere $300 or less in the late sixties once Buffett was at the helm, he or she would be a millionaire now from that small investment. At the time of this writing, those same ten shares have a stock market value of $3.4 million. It doesn't take a lot of money for you to achieve great wealth. It's just important that you get started investing now and let the power of compounding work for you.

Let me give you another proven example of just how effective dividend investing can be when the dividends are reinvested. Had you invested $10,000 in the S&P 500 Index in January of 1990 that investment would be worth roughly $92,000 today based on capital gains alone. Throw in the dividends that were received and reinvested and that investment would be worth a whopping $180,000 or double the return based on capitals gains alone. Every time you reinvest dividends that you receive, it entitles you to larger dividend payments—producing a snowball effect and turbocharging your returns in the future.

Following are two examples to allow you to see the difference between a fixed return on an investment of $10,000 with the annual dividends not reinvested and that same investment with the annual dividends reinvested for a compound return.

Example 1

Original Investment Amount: $10,000

Annual Return Percentage: 10%

(Dividends Not Reinvested)

YEAR	1	2	3	4	5	6	7	8	9	10
PROFIT	$1000	$1000	$1000	$1000	$1000	$1000	$1000	$1000	$1000	$1000

Total Profit: $10,000

Original Investment: $10,000

Ending Balance: $20,000

Example 2

Original Investment Amount: $10,000

Annual Return Percentage: 10%

(Dividends Reinvested)

YEAR	1	2	3	4	5	6	7	8	9	10
PROFITS	$11000	$12100	$13300	$14641	$16105	$17716	$19487	$21436	$23579	$25937

Total Profit: $15,937

Original Investment: $10,000

Ending Balance: $25,937

By reinvesting all dividends, an investor would end up with $5,937 or about 30% more money than he or she would have if the profits had not been reinvested. The power of compounding becomes even more potent over a longer period of time and when an investment's returns are greater. You want to make the dividend reinvesting process automatic; meaning once dividends are received, the brokerage or account manager will automatically reinvest those dividends into more shares of the company paying the dividend. Today, most brokerages offer something known as a Dividend Reinvestment Program or DRIP. In addition, most brokerages allow for the purchase of fractional shares. Until recently it was uncommon, except in the mutual fund industry, to find brokerages that would allow for the purchase of fractional shares.

The good news is that there are now many reputable brokerages that offer DRIPs along with the ability of investors to purchase fractional shares of stocks and exchange-traded funds (ETFs). Without the ability to purchase fractional shares, the investor would have to wait until he or she has enough funds in his or her account before being able to purchase certain stocks.

For example, let's say an investor contributes 10% of his base pay to his Individual Retirement Account (IRA) pretax and the 10% amounts to $60 weekly or about $240 monthly. The investor wants to build a position in iShares U.S. Medical Devices ETF—an exchange-traded fund that closed at a trading price of $318.63 at the time of writing this chapter. If the shares continue to trade at that price for the next few months, it will take the investor that contributes $60 weekly to his IRA about seven weeks before he has enough funds available to purchase just one share of iShares U.S. Medical Devices ETF. So, as you can see, there is an advantage to being able to purchase fractional shares.

I use TD Ameritrade and Merrill Edge for all of my investment accounts and think that both are great brokerages, but my use of them is certainly not an endorsement that you should do the same. Some other brokerages that offer Dividend Reinvestment Programs along with the ability to purchase fractional shares are Vanguard, Charles Schwab, T. Rowe Price, and Fidelity Investments. No doubt, there are also other reputable brokerages that offer DRIPs along with the ability to purchase fractional shares. The choice of brokerage is up to you. I want to also mention that most brokerages do not charge a fee or commission to buy equities, which is a very recent change. Whether you buy one share or one hundred shares, it cost you nothing. Now, that's a price that I love to pay.

5

IMPORTANT INVESTMENT FACTS

When it comes to stock market investing, what you know or don't know can make you or break you, literally. It is very important to know the facts when investing in stocks because not knowing the facts will likely lead to poor investment decisions and poor investment choices; which will likely lead to poor investment returns or losses. In this section, I address risk, stock market volatility, recessions, margin accounts, and stock splits since it seems that many individual investors have the greatest misconception about these concepts and should at least a basic understanding of them.

RISK: There are very few investments that are completely free from risk, because frankly all stock market investing carries some degree of risk. The main risk is the loss of your hard-earned money. So, the next time someone tries to push some sort of risk-free investment, you should be very suspicious. Your goal as an investor should be to reduce risk as much as possible. This is not achieved by picking safe, conservative stocks, but by picking stocks of outstanding companies and buying those stocks at the right price, and selling them when it becomes necessary.

STOCK MARKET VOLATILITY: A stock's price may fluctuate greatly within a short period of time even though nothing has fundamentally changed about the business. There are times when the stock market is calm and there are times when it's very volatile. Volatility is a normal process in the functioning of the stock market and should be expected. Stock market volatility is really a reflection of the investors' perception of what is going on with the economy. Successful investors understand that the stocks they buy may fall 50% or more in value, but they know not to panic and sell their shares in the process. Instead, they continue to focus on investing for the long-term. Getting scared out of the market is what keeps most people from making any sizable returns.

RECESSIONS: During recessions, most investors flee from stocks and move their money into what they consider safe havens such as U.S. Treasuries, high-grade bonds, money market accounts, and cash. What they fail to realize is that recessions and other economic woes are usually the best time to purchase stocks. Usually at some point during a recession, most stocks will trade at prices far less than they are worth. I'm referring to their intrinsic value or fair value when I speak of worth. Not surprisingly, you may find stocks trading at just 20-25% of their intrinsic value. When it comes to investment value, it does not get any better than finding deals like that.

MARGIN ACCOUNTS: A margin account is a credit line provided to you by your broker to use for investment purposes; the amount of the credit line is based on the value of your brokerage account. Most margin accounts allow you to have a credit line equal to the balance in your brokerage account. For example, let's say that you have $10,000 in your brokerage account. The margin account will usually allow you to purchase up to $20,000 in stocks, mutual funds, or other investments offered on the stock exchange. This is one time that you should not use OPM, or other people's money. Never use a margin account for investing in the stock market, and my reason for recommending that you don't is a good one. Stocks are too volatile over the short-term. With margin accounts, you can lose money even on excellent stock choices because even excellent stocks will tumble in price. My greatest capital losses were the result of foolishly using a margin account, so stay away from them. Even some of the world's best investors have gotten themselves into trouble through the use of margin accounts.

STOCK SPLITS: By definition, a stock split is the division of a share of stock into more shares that leaves the total value of the shares unchanged. For example, if a company announces that it has an upcoming 2-for-1 stock split for its shares, that means that for every share that an investor owns, he or she will receive two new shares that replace the original share. In other words, 100 original shares become 200 new shares. Although the share price will change, the total value of the shares will not. When I was a novice and inexperienced with investing, I always chased after stocks that were about to split. The only thing a split does is lower the trading price of a stock. What really matters is the business itself and how it's performing. None of those stocks that split after my purchase performed any better after they split. Wall Street would have you to believe that splits are important, but they really are not. So, don't pursue stock splits because doing so is just a waste of time, and you definitely won't get any richer from the process.

6

WHAT'S A DIVIDEND TRAP

The dividend yield is one of the most important metrics to consider when researching dividend stocks, but a high yield doesn't mean a better investment. Many years ago, before I knew better, I was easily impressed with any company that paid hefty dividends to its shareholders and when I say hefty yields, I'm talking about yields usually above five percent. Needless to say, it didn't take me long to realize that there's nothing impressive about owning high-yield dividend stocks. After all a high-yield means nothing, if it's not sustainable or if the stock paying the high-yield loses half of its value.

Who wouldn't love to own companies that pay dividend yields of 10% or more? They do exist but any company offering a high-yield should be examined carefully to see whether it's financially sound and whether it will be able to maintain the high dividend yield over the long-term. With my purchase of some high-yielding dividend stocks many years ago, I didn't realize at the time that I was falling for the dividend trap. I bought those stocks based solely on their high dividend yields, which is something that an investor should never do.

A dividend trap is a high-yield dividend stock whose payout is unsustainable. There's an old saying, "If something sounds too good to be true, it probably is." This saying is especially applicable when investing in high-yield dividend stocks.

Some troubled companies will pay high dividend yields in an effort to attract new investors with the hope that it will increase their stocks' trading prices. There are also stocks with high dividend yields that are the result of a decline in the stock's price. For example, if a company is trading at $100 per share and pays $5 per share in yearly dividends, the dividend yield would be 5%. If that same company maintains its dividend yield but its stock falls in price to $50 per share, its dividend yield would no longer be 5%, but its new yield would jump to 10%. A high dividend yield probably won't mean much to you when your stock has lost 50% of its value. When there is a rise in dividend yields because of a decline in the overall stock market, that's normal and should be expected because a falling stock price equals a higher yield for dividend-paying stocks. Remember to always determine why a stock has fallen in price anyway since a little extra insurance certainly won't hurt.

A major clue that a stock might be a dividend trap is when the company's dividend yield is much higher than other companies in its industry. If most companies in an industry pay dividend yields in the range of 2-3% but you have found a company in the same industry paying a much higher and more exciting yield of 10%, be very careful about investing in it. A company that pays out most of what it earns is highly likely to get itself into financial trouble and probably won't be able to maintain its dividend payments.

A dividend trap is something that all dividend investors need to watch out for. Remember, if it sounds too good to be true, it probably is!

7

DIVIDEND ARISTOCRATS

To write a book about dividend investing without discussing the Dividend Aristocrats would be a very unintelligent thing to do. Dividend Aristocrats are companies listed on the S&P 500 that have increased their annual dividend payment for at least 25 consecutive years, but most have increased their dividend payment for more than 40 consecutive years. There are some other criteria that must be met for a company to be listed as a Dividend Aristocrat, and they are (1) the company must have a minimum float-adjusted market capitalization (market cap.) of $3 billion and (2) the company's daily share trading value must average $5 million or more for the prior three months.

The list and number of Dividend Aristocrats does change infrequently with companies being added or removed from the list. Just think, any company that has managed to increase its annual dividend for more than 25 consecutive years has performed an amazing feat considering all the turmoil that the economy and the stock market experiences during almost any 25 years stretch.

Depending on your investment needs, the Dividend Aristocrats' list can be a great place to start when researching dividend stocks to include in your dividend portfolio since the companies are likely to be financially sound, possess durable competitive advantages within their industries, and have proven to be very reliable when it comes to their payment of dividends to shareholders. Any investor with the desire to own the entire Dividend Aristocrats list can do so through the purchase of ProShares S&P 500 Dividend Aristocrats ETF. The ETF is low-cost, offers low volatility and an above-average dividend yield.

8

HOW TO PICK WINNING DIVIDEND STOCKS

Before purchasing any dividend stock, the investor should look at several metrics or criteria to determine **(1)** if the company is financially solid with a long-term, sustainable competitive advantage **(2)** if the company has the ability to continue to consistently pay the dividend **(3)** if the company will be able to consistently grow its dividend long-term and **(4)** if the company's stock shares are still a good investment to own even if the company paid no dividends. I look for certain metrics or measures to be met before I invest my money into any stock including dividend stocks.

All too often some people will invest a lot of money into stocks, the stock market, or other investments without doing any sort of research or without using some type of established investment strategy. Why do they do it? The answer is they are trying to make some "fast money." Dividend stock investing is not a strategy for making fast money, but it will likely make you some money and lots of it if you continue to invest consistently over the long-term. Before we get into the metrics of what to look for in winning dividend stocks, I want to leave you with a thought from the legendary investor, Peter

Lynch. As Lynch has said, 'If you want to double your money quickly, fold it in half and put it back in your pocket."

Let's look now at the metrics for picking winning dividend stocks for your investment portfolio. I have outlined a seven-step process that I use to choose dividend stocks for my own portfolio. Some steps in the process are as simple as looking at the financial information for the company at a financial website such as FINVIZ to get the information that's needed. Some of the steps will require a little more work on your part, but the time spent will be worth it since it's going to help you avoid troubled companies and pick the best stocks for your dividend portfolio.

STEP ONE. **Verify that the company that you are interested in is a U.S. or Canadian company with a market capitalization of at least $2 billion.**

If you are new to dividend investing, it's best to stick with U.S. and Canadian companies until you have gained some experience as an investor. Although I'm a very experienced investor, I stay away from most foreign stocks especially Chinese and Indian companies. The laws in those countries are less stringent when it comes to the stock market and you never know what's going to happen with many of the foreign stocks. I lost a good sum of money investing in both Indian and Chinese stocks. To make matters even scarier, I did a great deal of research on the companies before investing only to find out that they were cooking the books—meaning they were manipulating financial data to make things look better than they really were. Also, stay away from small companies that are much riskier than larger companies. As a dividend investor, stay with companies that have a market capitalization of $2 billion or more.

STEP TWO. Check the P/E ratio of the company to see if it's forward P/E ratio is 20 or below.

There are exceptions to this ratio. If the company is growing fast, a higher P/E ratio may be warranted, but try to stick with those large, well-established, financially solid companies that tend to trade at P/E's of 20 or less. Purchasing a stock trading at a P/E of 20 or less, hopefully, will keep you from paying too much for a stock. There's absolutely nothing wrong with paying a fair price for a stock, but I never want to pay too much for a stock, and neither should you.

STEP THREE. Verify that the payout ratio percentage is 50% or less based on the company's earnings.

If a company is paying out most of what it earns in the form of dividends, it's likely to get itself into financial trouble. The lower the payout ratio, the more sustainable the yield should be. According to research, most experts believe that companies that maintain a payout ratio of 50% or less are much more likely to be capable of not only maintaining the dividend but growing it annually, and that's what we should want as dividend investors; a dividend that only gets sweeter with time. While it's getting sweeter, we are getting richer!

STEP FOUR. Check the company's debt to see if it reasonable for the company or if it's comparable to the debt of other companies in its industry.

Debt is an essential component in the operations of most businesses, but too much debt can be bad for a business. Too much debt reduces a business's profits, reduces the amount of money available for product research and development, and puts a business at greater risk of failure during a downturn in the economy. Use the debt-to-equity ratio to determine whether or not a company's debt is reasonable or if its debt levels are too high. As a general rule-of-thumb, look to invest in companies that carry a debt-to-equity ratio of 1 or less, but this rule should not be applied to all companies because many financially solid companies have debt-to-equity ratios higher than 1, and some have ratios that are much higher. So, an effective method is to look at the annual debt-to-equity ratios of a company for the last 7-10 years and determine what the company's long-term average annual debt-to-equity ratio is. Compare this average to the company's current debt-to-equity ratio. Let's look at the historical debt-to-equity ratios for the CSX Corporation for a better understanding of how to use the debt-to-equity ratio.

CSX CORPORATION (CSX) DEBT-EQUITY-RATIO 2008-2017

YEAR	2008	2009	2010	2011	2012	2013	2014	2015	2016	2017
DEBT TO EQUITY	0.93	0.89	0.93	1.03	1.01	0.86	0.85	0.92	0.94	0.80

From the information provided above, you will find that CSX Corporation average annual long-term debt-to-equity ratio is 0.92 and according to the report from which the company's current information was obtained, CSX Corporation currently has a debt-to-equity ratio of 1. Based on the company's historical debt-to-equity ratios, I would say that its current debt-to-equity ratio of 1 is very reasonable and acceptable for the company.

STEP FIVE. Check to see if the company has consistent annual increases in its earnings per share (EPS) over the long-term.

Look at the business's earnings per share for at least the last 7-10 years to determine if the earnings have increased consistently. Consistent increases in earnings per share tell us that a business is soundly managed. For dividend stocks, look for increases in earnings per share of 5% or more annually because as earnings increase, so should the stock's dividend and trading price. Let's look at the earnings of Dollar General Corporation and the earnings of PriceSmart, Inc. so that you can see exactly what to look for when it comes to consistent increases in earnings per share. Let's compare their earnings history for 10 years from 1999 to 2008.

DOLLAR GENERAL CORPORATION (DG) EARNINGS PER SHARE 2010-2019

YEAR	2010	2011	2012	2013	2014	2015	2016	2017	2018	2019
EPS	1.04	1.82	2.22	2.85	3.17	3.49	3.95	4.43	5.63	5.97

PRICESMART INC. (PSMT) EARNINGS PER SHARE 2010-2019

YEAR	2010	2011	2012	2013	2014	2015	2016	2017	2018	2019
EPS	1.65	2.07	2.24	2.78	3.07	2.95	2.92	2.98	2.44	2.40

Dollar General Corporation has what is considered to be a perfect earnings history because it has managed to grow its earnings consistently every year for the ten-year period covered. Its performance has been impressive, and it would be an excellent dividend stock when purchased at the right price if it meets all the metrics described. As a dividend investor, you want to own businesses with consistent earnings like those of Dollar General. PriceSmart, Inc. earnings per share are not increasing consistently but actually decreased in the last two years covered in the report. As a dividend investor, I would not bother buying shares of PriceSmart, Inc. since its earnings are not consistently increasing, and recommend that you stick with companies that have a history of consistent increases in earnings like those of Dollar General. Great companies like Dollar General will more than likely make you a lot of money over the long term. Of course, there are exceptions to this rule. For example, if the economy is experiencing a recession, the company being researched may not show consistent earnings during that period since the majority of businesses tend to suffer during recessions.

STEP SIX. Verify that the business has a five-year history of consistently high returns on equity, also known as the ROE.

A high return on equity is an essential element of top-performing stocks. The return on equity is a gauge of a business's profitability and it also serves as management's report card. The return on equity, like the retained earnings, tells us whether management is effectively using profits to increase shareholders' equity. Favor stocks with an average return on equity of 10% or more over the most recent 5-year period.

The return on equity also tells us whether a business has a competitive advantage in its industry and a competitive advantage is to be desired. Let's return to the comparison between Dollar General Corporation and PriceSmart, Inc. We will look at their returns on equity from 2016 through 2020.

DOLLAR GENERAL CORP. (DG) RETURNS ON EQUITY 2016-2020

YEAR	2016	2017	2018	2019	2020
ROE	21.0%	23.2%	26.7%	25.3%	26.1%

PRICESMART INC. (PSMT) RETURNS ON EQUITY 2016-2020

YEAR	2016	2017	2018	2019	2020
ROE	14.5%	13.3%	10.0%	9.3%	9.5%

When looking at PriceSmart, Inc. you will see that its returns on equity have been very inconsistent and actually decreasing. It would be hard for me to place any confidence in the stock's future performance because of its inconsistent history. It's ok if returns on equity are lower than 12% during some time periods, but they should be consistent and average out at 12% or more over the most recent five-year period plus those returns on equity need to be consistent or gradually increasing. When looking at Dollar General Corporation, it consistently had very high returns on equity and if you average out its return on equity for the period shown, you will find that it had a five-year average return on equity of 24.5%. What's even more impressive is the fact that it had high and consistent returns on equity for the most recent 10-year period reported.

STEP SEVEN. The business must have a positive free cash flow for each year for the most recent three-year period.

Although earnings can be easily manipulated, it's much harder for a business to manipulate its cash flow statement. A positive free cash flow is a further confirmation that the business is financially sound, and it also demonstrates management's ability to make money for the business and its investors. I could have easily established more stringent free cash flow requirements, but feel that a positive cash flow for the most recent three years should suffice.

Dollar General Corporation

Year	Free Cash Flow
2018	1.2 Billion
2019	1.4 Billion
2020	1.5 Billion

As you can see from the table above, Dollar General Corporation easily met the requirement of having a positive free cash flow for every year for the most recent three-year period. Many professional investors rely on a company's earnings when making various investment decisions although a smart accountant or financial officer can easily manipulate earnings. Cash flow information is much harder to manipulate. When a company is capable of producing positive free cash flows consistently, it's a good sign that the company is making money and if the company is making money, it should be able to pay its investors with a dividend that's growing and that only gets better with time.

It's okay to make minor exceptions to some of the requirements set forth here because when it comes to dividend investing, nothing is written in stone, but it is best to stay within the bounds of the criteria that is presented here if you are just starting out on this journey which can be rewarding and can put you on a path to financial freedom that you never thought was possible. The stocks that were used in the examples were for informational purpose only and financial information will have changed with all of them before this book is published.

I believe that the seven-step process for picking winning dividend stocks will allow the dividend investor to build a portfolio of solid performing dividend stocks that will do well over the long-term.

If you have not done so already, get your free gift as my way of thanking you for purchasing my book! Click below to receive my free report.

5 STOCKS THAT WARREN BUFFETT WOULD LOVE

https://mailchi.mp/b65776af6219/5-stocks-warren-buffett-would-love

9

DIVIDEND STOCKS BUY STRATEGIES

When purchasing dividend stocks, I think the best manner to do so is the same as an investor would, using a strategy that looks for value in common stock purchases. I have often been asked about the best strategy or method an investor should use when building a stock's position within his or her portfolio. Some professionals think that the entire sum of money to be invested should be spent all at once with a one-time lump sum purchase. Still, other professionals believe that an investor should gradually build a position for each company that is purchased using dollar-cost averaging or by splitting up the purchases. Here's a definition of dollar-cost averaging:

The process of investing a fixed amount or percentage of money into an investment at regular intervals regardless of the investment's cost.

According to research, lump-sum investing will usually produce a higher return than dollar-cost averaging about 7 times out of 10. The drawback to investing a lump sum into a particular investment is that the investment could experience a significant drop in price soon after its purchase. I must admit that I'm no stranger to such an event happening to me on many occasions.

For example, many years ago I spent a lump sum of more than $5000 buying shares of First Marblehead Corporation only to watch the stock tumble in price, turning my investment into less than $2000 in only a few weeks. Over the course of a few months, I lost every penny of my money on that investment. So, I'm not a big fan of the strategy of investing a lump sum into an individual stock when building its position within my portfolio.

Dollar-cost averaging, unlike investing a lump sum, reduces the risk of investing a large amount of money into an investment at the wrong time, and through its use, an investor will buy more shares at lower prices and fewer shares when prices are higher. There has been a considerable amount of controversy concerning dollar-cost averaging, but I believe that it is especially useful for employees that invest through 401Ks and other types of employer-sponsored retirement plans._ Once the retirement account is set up, the employer deducts contributions from the employee's check during each pay period, which makes the process automatic and makes it easier for even the undisciplined saver to build wealth.

Another advantage to dollar-cost averaging is the fact that it allows an individual to invest small sums of money into the stock market since most individuals probably don't have large sums of money to invest. In time, the investor that sticks to a steady plan of dollar-cost averaging is likely to have a substantial nest egg when the time comes to retire. I also believe that dollar-cost averaging is a good strategy to use when purchasing mutual funds, bonds funds, index funds, and exchange-traded funds, and some other types of securities. With those types of securities, some type of estimate of value is usually not an issue for the investor; however, identifying value is at the heart of successful, long-term investing in individual stocks.

Although I'm for dollar-cost averaging, I don't believe that it should be used to purchase dividend stocks or by those who purchase individual stocks as long-term investments. It's best to buy dividend stocks when they are trading at their estimated trading price or at a discount to their estimated trading price that will be explained a little later. I like the method that Jim Cramer, an investment genius and the host of *Mad Money,* uses to build his positions when investing in individual stocks although I use a slightly modified version of his method.

I use to think that it was quite ridiculous to build a position in a stock by spreading purchases out over a few periods instead of one lump sum investment because I believed that the individuals that bought in such a manner really didn't know the value of what they were buying. I gladly admit that I was wrong in my belief. Especially, after watching some of my lump sum investments drop significantly in value shortly after my purchase.

In Cramer's book, *Jim Cramer's Get Rich Carefully,* he stresses the importance of an investor splitting his or her purchases up when starting a position in a new stock. He says that doing so gives an investor the opportunity to lower his cost basis with each purchase. Let's put it another way, he believes that every time an investor purchase shares of a specific stock, he or she should attempt to purchase those shares cheaper, thereby, lowering the average cost per share that is paid for the shares.

Before I make my second and third purchase, I like to wait to see if the stock will drop a few more dollars although I'm willing to pay my purchase price, which has already been determined in advance. It may mean waiting a few weeks or months before buying more shares. If the stock falls a few more dollars, I buy more shares and if it does not, I will still buy more shares for my portfolio as long as I'm able to purchase the shares at my desired price. If I'm unable to build a sizeable position of a stock in my portfolio because the stock becomes too expensive, I continue to hold onto the smaller lot as I would any other shares and will usually only sell my shares in accordance to sell rules that I have established for myself. It's as simple as that for me.

I believe that the investor that split his purchases up and buys more shares of a stock when he or she is able to lower the cost basis of the shares with each purchase is investing wisely since doing so will lower the average cost per share each times shares are added to the portfolio. A lump-sum purchase of our shares will leave us with no wiggle room to lower our average cost per share if the shares were to drop in price. Splitting our purchases up over three to four buy periods is the best way to buy common stock shares or dividend stock shares, and I think that more money will be made and less will be lost during the process.

10

KEEP YOUR PORTFOLIO SMALL

Even among the investment professionals, opinions vary about the optimal number of stocks that a portfolio should contain, and most individual investors are not sure about how many stocks to hold in their portfolio for the best performance and less risk. If you are just starting out with a small amount of money to invest, the number of stocks contained in your portfolio won't matter much but as your portfolio grows in value, the numbers of stocks held in it do matter.

Robert Hagstrom, the author of *The Warren Buffett Portfolio,* has performed extensive research into portfolio management. As he states in *The Warren Buffett Portfolio*, "Your probability of beating the market goes up as the size of your portfolio goes down. With a 15-stock portfolio, you have a 1-in-4 chance of beating the market. With a 250-stock portfolio, your chances are 1 in 50." Many years ago I did some research into the number of stocks contained in the portfolios of some of America's top money managers. I was only interested in those that had managed to obtain long-term returns above 15% and the results of my research are contained in the table that follows.

Although the information was obtained many years ago, we definitely can learn something from it.

Looking at the results in the table, we find that the long-term average annual rate of return for the portfolios listed was 23.3% and the average number of stocks in these winning portfolios was twelve when we exclude famed investor Robert Rodriquez who did an amazing job with a portfolio containing a much larger number of stocks than the average of 12 found in the portfolios of the other investors used in the comparison. When looking at their performance, it's pretty hard to argue against the results that these portfolios have achieved although most are concentrated in the number of stocks they contained.

INVESTOR'S NAME	STOCKS HELD	LONG -TERM PERFORMANCE
Ian Cumming	5	33% annually from 1978-2004
Glenn Greenberg	12	23% annually from 1984-2004
Robert Karr	9	22% annually from 1996-2010
Seth Klarman	17	20% annually from inception in 1983
Edward Lampert	11	29% annually from 1988-2009

Mohnish Pabrai	17	29% annually from 1999-2006
David Swenson	10	17% annually for last ten years based on the date of the article.
Robert Rodriquez	25-45	17% annually from 1984-2007
Lou Simpson	13	20% annually from 1980-2004

Dave Kansas, former editor-in-chief of *TheStreet.com,* once said, "For most people, the ability to follow more than a dozen stocks is likely limited. A portfolio of a dozen or so stocks should provide you with the protection of diversification and the focus to build wealth." Isn't it amazing that we have been conditioned to believe that more is better? As you can see, when it comes to investing in stocks, more can be detrimental instead of beneficial to a portfolio's performance. So, in reality, less is more when investing in individual stocks.

Jordan L. Kimmel, a leading investment expert and successful money manager, states in his book *Magnet Investing,* "It only requires a handful of long-term profits in outstanding companies to create personal independent wealth." In other words, he is saying that it only takes owning stock shares in a few outstanding companies over the long-term to become very wealthy.

After much study, I have concluded that a dividend stock portfolio should contain a minimum of 20 and a maximum of about 30 stocks.

I realize that the number is higher than the 15 stock portfolio recommended by Robert Hagstrom, but I believe that for the dividend investor, a portfolio of at least 20 stocks will allow for greater diversification while improving returns. Based on several studies, holding a portfolio of 20 stocks gives an investor nearly the same benefits as owning a much larger portfolio. In addition, 20 stocks will help smooth out investment returns by compensating for the bad picks that end up in the portfolio. Yes, I said that correctly. I don't care how good of a stock picker you may be, if you purchase 20 stocks, not all of them will be winners. If you don't already have the funds to invest all at once, you will have to do like I did with my very first portfolio and gradually work your way up to the 20 stocks minimum.

By following these recommendations, the dividend investor ends up with a portfolio that allows for good diversification and at the same time, the portfolio is not so large that the investor has a hard time monitoring the stocks. For the dividend investor, I believe that the portfolio should be equally weighted in each stock's position. When I say equally weighted, I mean that the investor should put an equal amount of money into each stock held within his or her portfolio. For example, if I had $100,000 to invest all at once, to invest it equally weighted, I would put $5000 into each stock if I were going to have the recommended minimum of 20 stocks.

Studies have shown that investors that keep their portfolios small improve their chances of beating the market. A winning dividend stock portfolio should contain a minimum of 20 and a maximum of about 30 stocks based on my research.

11

HOW TO VALUE A DIVIDEND STOCK

When looking at dividend stocks, I believe that the P/E ratio is the best tool to use to place some value or price on them. I think that it's a great tool for estimating what a dividend stock's trading price should be based on its past trading history. Many stock market pros rely on the P/E ratio as an important and vital investment tool and have achieved amazing success through its use. The P/E ratio is also a very useful measure for determining if a stock is overvalued or undervalued, expensive or cheap relative to the stock market as a whole and relative to other stocks within the same industry or sector.

When using the P/E ratio to estimate a dividend stock's trading price, I believe that the P/E ratio is especially helpful for use with very large companies, which tend to be dividend payers that are not growing very fast anymore. Companies such as Nike, Proctor & Gamble, Wal-Mart and Coca-Cola are huge businesses that are highly unlikely to grow their revenue and EPS at the higher rates they were capable of when they were much younger and smaller companies; yet, these are still excellent businesses to invest in at the right price.

Because of the size and slower growth rates of these large companies, some valuation methods will sometimes assign values that are too low for such wonderful, safe, and consistently performing businesses; and that's where the P/E ratio can be an effective remedy.

When using the P/E ratio, you should use the long-term average annual P/E ratio for better and more accurate estimates of a dividend stock's trading price. When we use the P/E ratio in the manner that's being shown here, we are not determining a stock's intrinsic value, but we are seeing, historically, what investors were willing to pay for a specific stock based on its EPS estimates and we are estimating the price they are likely to pay now or at some point in the future. Anytime the term "long-term" is used throughout this guide, it's referring to a period of 7 to 10 years. When referring to P/E ratio, if only a five-year history is available, I will use it but never less than five years for my estimates. Now, let's take a look at a few examples of how to use the P/E ratio to estimate a dividend stock's trading price.

We will look first at Automatic Data Processing, a provider of cloud-based human capital management solutions worldwide. The following table shows the average annual P/E ratios that Automatic Data Processing traded for from 2011 through 2020.

AUTOMATIC DATA PROCESSING (ADP) P/E RATIOS 2001-2010

YEAR	2011	2012	2013	2014	2015	2016	2017	2018	2019	2020
P/E	21.0	20.4	28.3	26.2	28.3	30.8	29.7	33.8	31.4	31.1

We must first determine the total of the P/E averages by adding the values given for all 10 years from 2011 through 2020. Once we have the total, we divide it by 10 to obtain our long-term average annual P/E ratio. The equation for Automatic Data Processing follows:

281.0 (Sum of P/E Averages) / 10 (Total Number of Years) = 28.1(Long-Term Avg. P/E Ratio)

Analysts estimate that Automatic Data Processing will earn $5.64 in 2021 and the stock traded at $179.24 per share at the time of this analysis in late December of 2020. To estimate the stock's trading price using the P/E ratio, you multiply the estimated EPS for 2021 by the long-term average P/E ratio. The equation would be as follows:

$5.64 (2021 EPS Estimate) x 28.1 (Long-Term Average P/E Ratio) = $158.48 (Estimated Trading Price).

Based on what investors were willing to pay in the past for Automatic Data Processing shares, the share should now trade for about $158.48 instead of the $179.24 that the shares trade for, meaning that Automatic Data Processing shares are overvalued and trading almost 14% higher than most investors have been willing to pay in the past for its shares. So, I would not buy Automatic Data Processing at its current trading price of $179.24, but would wait for the shares to fall to a more reasonable price before buying them.

Let's now take a look at AbbVie Inc. to estimate its trading price from the use of the P/E ratio. Its average annual P/E ratio history is contained in the following table:

ABBVIE INC. (ABBV) AVERAGE ANNUAL P/E RATIO 2012-2020

YEAR	2012	2013	2014	2015	2016	2017	2018	2019	2020
P/E	10.2	18.5	28.5	34.6	16.9	23.5	19.1	39.0	22.5

When we add the average annual P/E ratios up for the years shown, we find that our sum is 212.8 and we will need to divide the sum by the number of years for which the average annual P/E ratios are supplied, which is 9, to obtain our long-term average P/E ratio. Let's look next at the equation for AbbVie Inc.

212.8 (Sum of P/E Averages) / 9 (Total Number of Years) = 23.6 (Long-Term Avg. P/E Ratio)

Analysts estimated AbbVie Inc. would earn $12.22 per share in 2021 and the stock traded at $104.39 per share at the time of this analysis in late December of 2020. To estimate the stock's trading price using the P/E ratio, multiply the 2021 estimated EPS of $12.22 by the long-term average P/E ratio of 23.6. The equation would be as follows:

$12.22 (2021 EPS Estimate) x 23.6 (Long-Term Average P/E Ratio) = $288.39 (Estimated Trading Price).

Based on what investors were willing to pay in the past for AbbVie Inc., shares should be trading for about $288.39 but were trading at $104.39 at the time of this study, which means that AbbVie Inc. shares were trading for much less than investors have been willing to pay for its shares in the past based on the P/E ratio. The shares are trading for about 176% less than the estimated trading price of $288.39. So, I would take a serious look at the shares of Abbvie Inc. and consider adding shares to my dividend stock portfolio. When I use this method to determine my purchase price of a dividend stock, I still rely on a margin of safety just as I do with the other methods I use to perform various stock valuations. However with AbbVie, Inc. trading at such a big price difference, the margin of safety is already there.

As you can see, the P/E ratio and more specifically, the average annual P/E ratio (long-term) is a very useful measure for estimating a stock's trading price and it's simple to use. I especially think that it's a very useful measure when it comes to estimating the trading price of dividend stocks. When using measurements like this, it's much easier to determine when an investor should buy shares of a specific stock since he or she will have some idea of a trading price of the shares.

12

USING LIMIT ORDERS

There are several types of orders that can be placed when we buy or sell a stock but it's my belief that the individual or small investor needs only an understanding of two types and they are *market orders* and *limit orders*.

A market order is defined as an order to buy or sell a stock at the best available price. With market orders, the order is generally executed quickly but the drawback is that the price at which a market order will be executed is not guaranteed. In other words, when using market orders, it is possible to pay more for a stock share or receive less for a stock share than you desire.

A limit order is defined as an order to buy or sell a stock at a specific price or better. The drawback to using limit orders is they can only be filled if the stock market's price reaches the limit price and the numbers of shares desired are available for purchase. The advantage of using limit orders is that they prevent an investor from paying more than he or she desires for a stock being purchased and guarantee that he or she will receive the price desired or a better one for the stock that is being sold if the trade executes.

In the past, I have used both types of orders but now believe that an investor is always better off using limit orders when buying or selling shares of any stocks through his or her brokerage account. In my mind, placing or using market orders is a losing proposition and work to an investor's disadvantage. So, always use limit orders when buying and selling stocks. That way, the deal works in your favor instead of someone else's.

13

SELLING A DIVIDEND STOCK

Dividend Investing is long-term investing and the same sell strategies that apply to long-term investment strategies also apply to dividend investing. Determining when to sell a stock is much harder than determining when to buy one because sometimes a stock that appears to be overvalued can continue to rise in price for many years and can increase in value several thousand percentages from the original purchase price.

It's a fact that even the world's best investors wrestle with determining when to sell a stock and most will admit it's much easier to decide when to buy, than when to sell. Author Robert Hagstrom has written several excellent books about Warren Buffett and his investment strategies. In *The Warren Buffett Portfolio*, he says that an investor should leave his or her portfolio intact for at least five years, as long as the fundamentals for which a particular stock was purchased do not deteriorate. He also says investors should pay no attention to a stock's price volatility because it is a normal part of the investment cycle.

In their book *Million Dollar Portfolio*, the Motley Fool team says investors' minimum holding period for each stock that is purchased should be three to five years. As a long-term investor, there will be times when it makes sense to sell or reduce your position in a stock earlier than you had planned. Next, we will talk about different circumstances in which you should consider selling a stock or at the very least, reducing your position. Of course, these same sell strategies also apply when using any type of long-term investing strategy such as value investing.

When the Company Cancels or Reduces Its Dividend - When it comes to dividend investing, the dividend being canceled or reduced can mean bad news for the investor and might just be a good reason to sell the stock. Dividend cuts or reductions are usually a sign that the company is experiencing some financial challenges or see some financial difficulties in the near future. When dividend cuts or reductions arise, it's in the interest of the investor to find out what's going on. The issue might just be temporary or short-term such as unexpected one-time expenses, or something more serious such as weakening or deteriorating earnings.

The Time Frame - If you will need the money within five years, it should not be invested in stocks. It would be best to invest your money in safe and stable short-term instruments. Money market accounts, money market funds, and short-term certificates of deposits would be better options.

An Overvalued Stock - When a stock is significantly overvalued, sell it. Take the proceeds from the sale and invest them into other undervalued stocks that you have researched. The P/E ratio is still one of the best indicators of value. For example, if a stock has traded at an average P/E of 15 for the last 7 to 10 years and the business is thriving, but the stock currently trades at a P/E of 30 or more on consistent or increasing EPS, you might consider selling the stock or at least reducing its position within your portfolio.

For the large companies and dividend payers that I own in my dividend portfolio, I mainly rely on the P/E ratio to determine if a stock is a buy or sell and that metric has worked extremely well for me. I must admit, I'm slow to sell an overvalued stock if it's not extremely overvalued because excellent investment choices are hard to find; if they are in my portfolio, it's because I consider them to be excellent selections.

Too Much Debt - Too much debt is dangerous for any business because there's always the chance that a business may be unable to pay its debt. Too much debt also puts a business at greater risk of failure if a downturn in the industry or economy were to occur. Upon entering the 2007 recession, thousands of businesses here in the United States literally disappeared overnight and that was before things really got bad. I'm willing to bet that those businesses that were carrying too much debt were the first to go.

When looking at the debt of a company, I like to look at how the company has handled its debt over the long-term. For example, I will look at its annual debt-to-equity ratios for the last ten years. If the company has managed to keep its debt-to-equity ratio within a specific range and all of a sudden its ratio moves way above that range, I will take a serious look at the company to try to determine what's going on. Normally, I like companies with debt-to-equity ratios of 1.00 or less but that rule cannot be applied to all companies. There are many solid and financially sound companies that carry debt-to-equity ratios that are much higher. So, it's also a good idea to look at a company's historical debt-to-equity ratios over the last 7 to 10 years to see if it's normal or if it's out of the ordinary.

Too Much Risk - Sometimes new management will come to a business and begin to implement new policies; along with that implementation, they will knowingly or unknowingly expose a business to greater risk. If you purchased the stock of a company that stayed away from very risky practices, but the company has now begun to display risky behaviors that make you uncomfortable, sell the stock and find yourself a better investment.

Loss of Competitive Advantage - You have also learned that we should only be purchasing the stocks of companies that have a durable competitive advantage. When a company changes its business model, resulting in it losing its competitive advantage, sell the stock. Having a durable competitive advantage is essential to any stock that you purchase using a dividend investing strategy.

The Portfolio Lacks Balance or Diversification - It's very easy for your best performing stock to become the largest holding in your portfolio, and there's absolutely nothing wrong with that. The problem arises when the stock makes up more than 20-25% of your portfolio's total value. I would be very uncomfortable having more than 25% of my portfolio's value tied to just one stock. Legendary investor, Jim Slater suggests that individual investors limit the number of funds invested in a single stock within their portfolios to a maximum of 15%. When your portfolio becomes heavily weighted in one stock, consider reducing your position of that stock to bring more balance and better diversification into your portfolio.

When Your Analysis is Found to Be Flawed- There will be times when an investor will be very detailed and careful in his or her analysis of a particular company or its stock, only to find out later that his or her analysis is incorrect or flawed. Whether a stock should be sold at that time depends on the seriousness of the error and its impact on the long-term performance of the business. So, when you find that you have incorrectly analyzed a particular company, it is essential for you to look at all available information to determine whether or not to sell the stock or to continue holding it. One thing is certain, as an investor, you will not always be right when analyzing a company or its stock.

14

THE STOCK SCREENER

When it comes to investing, things can get a little complex, especially when it comes to identifying the right stocks for your portfolio. Consider the fact that there are three major stock exchanges in the United States with no less than 2400 stocks listed on the New York Stock Exchange alone, and each of those companies that the stocks represent are different in their makeup. For example, their business prospects, their employees, their facilities, and their finances will be very different, and this only complicates the matter for investors. Don't forget, we have not even included the companies that trade on the other two major exchanges here in the United States. If that's not enough to making picking stocks more complex, I don't know what is.

The stock screener is an excellent tool for identifying potential investment candidates, by making the process less convoluted. A stock screener is a very powerful investment tool that scans a database to search for stocks that meet certain criteria, which have been specified by an investor. The main components of any screener are a database of companies (stocks), a set of variables, and a screening engine that functions much like a search engine on the Internet.

Screeners may vary from being very simple and basic, to much more complex. However, good screeners will allow investors to search for companies using just about any criterion that's desired. Stock screeners may be standalone software programs or web-based programs. I use only the free, web-based screeners, and I think that a few of them are excellent, and several of the web-based screeners are free to use.

I have spent thousands of hours researching and studying stocks. The truth is that much of that time could have been put to better use if only I had known about stock screeners when I started my research many years ago. With stock screeners, investors are capable of analyzing hundreds of stocks in a very short time. This same process of analyzing stocks usually would have taken days or even weeks to perform before stock screeners were available, and that's no exaggeration! Stock screeners save time by quickly eliminating those companies that do not meet an investor's requirements.

15

HOW TO USE THE FINVIZ SCREENER TO FIND WINNING DIVIDEND STOCKS

https://finviz.com/screener.ashx

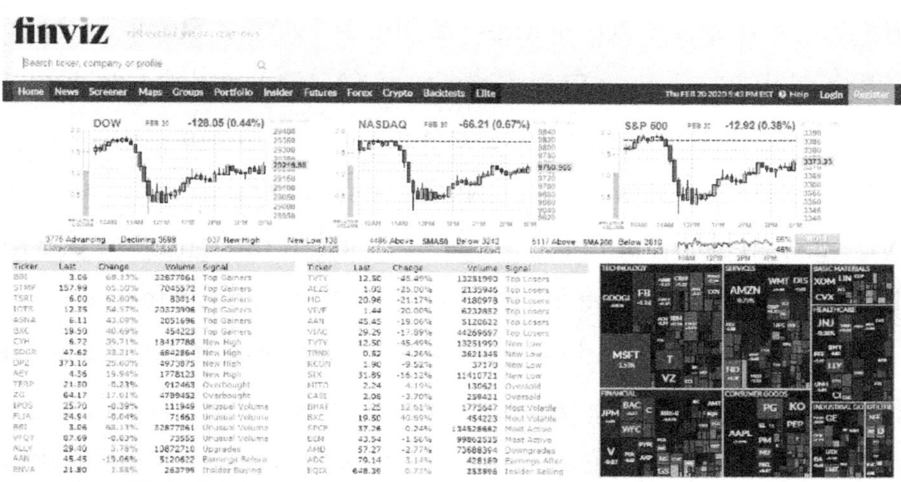

When searching for winning dividend stocks for my portfolio, the FINVIZ stock screener is my favorite. The FINVIZ stock screener is an online, browser-based stock screening tool that allows users to screen for stocks using a wide variety of descriptive, fundamental, and technical filters. The FINVIZ platform offers free and premium tools that traders and investors can use to generate stock investing ideas. I use only the free screening tool, and it easily meets my investment needs. The FINVIZ screener can be applied to many different trading or investing strategies and is a very useful tool for both new and experienced investors.

With a little familiarization, most users will find the FINVIZ platform to be user-friendly. The platform provides a sector performance tool, portfolio tracking, various charts and graphs, and numerous other features, which users may find valuable. The FINVIZ screener contains approximately 7,700 stocks in its database. In addition to stocks, users can analyze specific sectors or indexes. Users should be aware that quotes received through the FINVIZ platform are delayed 20 minutes for the New York Stock Exchange (NYSE) and the American Stock Exchange (AMEX), and are delayed 15 minutes for the Nasdaq Stock Exchange unless users purchase the premium services offered by FINVIZ. First-time users can use the FINVIZ website without being required to log in or sign up to use the website, but will only have access to the website's basic features.

To access the more advanced features, the user must register on the website, which is a very simple and quick process. Users can also sign up for FINVIZ's Elite Plan, which is the paid version. With it, users gain access to premium features not available to free or registered users. To use the FINVIZ screener, you simply select or enter your desired criteria into the different filters available in the screener. The FINVIZ screener contains predefined selections for the filters and it's up to you, the investor, to select the criteria that you desire companies to meet.

I have provided the criteria that I use when searching for dividend stocks for my personal portfolio to give you an idea of how the FINVIZ screener works. Go to the FINVIZ screener and enter my research criteria and see what stocks (companies) the screener retrieves. Once you have done so, you can then enter your desired criteria that you want stocks to meet. It's as simple as that. My stock screen looks for high-quality companies with durable competitive advantages that pay dividends. The screener also looks for companies with low-debt that are financially sound.

HIGH-QUALITY DIVIDEND STOCKS SCREEN

Country: USA

Market Capitalization: +Mid (Over $2 Billion)

Forward P/E: Under 20

Sales Growth (Past 5 Years): Positive (Greater than 0)

Dividend Yield: Over 3%

Payout Ratio: Under 60

Return on Equity: Over +10%

Debt/Equity Ratio: Under 1.0

The FINVIZ screener will generate a list of stocks that will need to be further studied and is merely the first step. But, it is a very important step since it filters out stocks that don't meet your required criteria, and creates a list of stocks that do. Screeners and stock screening should never be used as substitutes for performing your research. The stocks retrieved by a screener or screening tool should not be considered a buy list, but a thorough financial analysis should be performed on every stock before determining whether or not to purchase them. Also, keep in mind that the screening criteria that has been presented here is my own and it's up to you to decide what criteria is needed based on your own investing program or strategy. Once you begin to create your own customized screens with the FINVIZ stock screener, you can save those screens so that when you decide to perform stock research at a later date, you only have to log in to your FINVIZ account and pull up the screen that was saved along with all of the required search criteria.

16

10 GREAT DIVIDEND STOCKS FOR THE LONG RUN

The author or publisher is not engaged in rendering legal, accounting, investment, or other professional services. Investing in stocks and the stock market involves varying degrees of risk, and there's no assurance that a specific stock, investment principle, or investment strategy will be profitable for an individual, group, or organization. Although the 10 Stocks listed in this section may meet certain criteria set forth in this book, it's not a recommendation from the author or publisher to purchase or sell any of the stocks discussed herein. A stock's past performance does not guarantee similar future results.

All information contained in this book was gathered from sources believed to be reliable, but neither the author nor the publisher can accept responsibility for its accuracy. The author or publisher specifically disclaim any responsibility for liability, loss, or risk, professional or otherwise, which is incurred as a consequence, directly or indirectly, of the use and application of any of the contents of this book. All financial data for the 10 stocks presented is as of January 22, 2021.

AbbVie, Inc. #1

NYSE	ABBV
Industry	Drug Manufacturers-General
Sector	Healthcare
Employees	47,000 (Full Time)
Website	www.abbvie.com

AbbVie, Inc. is a global biopharmaceutical company. The company is engaged in the discovery, development, and commercialization of a wide range of pharmaceutical products, and sells its products throughout the world. The company lists its products under several categories: Immunology, Neuroscience, Oncology, Virology, and General Medicine.

AbbVie, Inc. has grown its earnings per share (EPS) at an annual rate of 36.8% during its most recent five-year period. The company achieved an average annual return on equity (ROE) of 117.9% from 2013 through 2017 but experienced negative returns on equity for 2018 and 2019. Its return on equity for its trailing twelve months stands at 208%. The company achieved an average annual return on capital (ROC) of 17.5% from 2013 through 2017 but experienced negative returns on capital for 2018 and 2019. Its return on capital for its trailing twelve months stands at 14.0%.
The company has a debt-to-equity ratio of 5.70 and is expected to grow its earnings per share at an annual rate of 11.0% over the long-term. The company currently pays an annual dividend of 4.85%.

AbbVie, Inc. was founded on October 19, 2011 and is headquartered in North Chicago, IL.

Bank of America Corporation #2

NYSE	BAC
Industry	Banks-Diversified
Sector	FinancialServices
Employees	211,000 (Full Time)
Website	www.bankofamerica.com

Bank of America Corporation is one of the largest financial institutions in the United States and one of the world's leading financial institutions. The company serves approximately 66 million consumers and small business clients, having approximately 4,300 retail financial centers. The company has four major segments: Consumer Banking, Global Banking, Global Markets, and Global Wealth and Investment Management. The company serves clients throughout the United States, its territories, and 35 countries.

Bank of America has grown its earnings per share (EPS) at an annual rate of 45.5% during its most recent five-year period. The company has achieved an average annual return on equity (ROE) of 8.3% and an average annual return on Assets (ROA) of 0.88% during the last five years. The company has a debt-to-equity ratio of 1.11. The company is expected to grow its earnings per share at an annual rate of 7.0% over the long-term. Bank of America Corporation currently pays an annual dividend of 2.21%.

The company, Inc. was founded in 1784 and is headquartered in Charlotte, North Carolina.

Bristol-Myers Squibb Company #3

NYSE	BMY
Industry	Drug Manufacturers-General
Sector	Healthcare
Employees	30,000 (Full Time)
Website	www.bms.com

Bristol-Myers Squibb Company is a global biopharmaceutical company. It discovers, develops, and commercializes innovative medicines that treat patients with serious diseases. It offers products for a range of therapeutic classes including hematology, oncology, cardiovascular, and immunology. Its products are sold to retail pharmacies, wholesalers, hospitals, government entities, and medical professionals worldwide. The company is studying more than 40 disease areas and has more than 50 compounds in development.

Bristol-Myers Squibb Company has grown its earnings per share (EPS) at an annual rate of 10.9% during its most recent five-year period. The company has achieved an average annual return on equity (ROE) of 19.2% and an average annual return on capital (ROC) of 13.0% during the last five years. The company has a debt-to-equity ratio of 0.90 and is expected to grow its earnings per share at an annual rate of 21.4% over the long-term. Bristol-Myers Squibb currently pays an annual dividend of 3.02%.

The company was founded in 1887 and is headquartered in New York, New York.

The Clorox Company #4

NYSE	CLX
Industry	Household & Personal Products
Sector	Consumer Defensive
Employees	8,800 (Full Time)
Website	www.thecloroxcompany.com

The Clorox Company is a manufacturer and marketer of consumer and professional products worldwide. The company markets some of the most recognized brands in the world and its products are primarily sold through grocery stores and other retail stores. The Clorox Company operates through four segments: Household, Health and Wellness, Lifestyle, and International. For fiscal year 2020, the company had sales of $6.7 billion.

The Clorox Company has grown its earnings per share (EPS) at an annual rate of 10.0% during its most recent five-year period. The company has achieved an average annual return on equity (ROE) of 173.0% and an average annual return on capital (ROC) of 28.5% during the last five years. The company has a current ratio of 1.4 and a debt-to-equity ratio of zero. The Clorox Company is expected to grow its earnings per share at an annual rate of 4.9% over the long-term and currently pays an annual dividend of 2.29%.

The company was founded in 1913 and is headquartered in Oakland, California.

CVS Health Corp. #5

NYSE	CVS
Industry	Health Care Plans
Sector	Healthcare
Employees	290,000 (Full Time)
Website	www.cvshealth.com

CVS Health Corp. together is the largest pharmacy health care provider in the U.S. with more than 9,900 retail locations in 49 states, the District of Columbia, and Puerto Rico. It also has more than 1,100 MinuteClinic locations in 33 states and the District of Columbia.

CVS Health offers affordable health services such as in-store dietitian counseling services, immunization services, medical examinations, physicals, and blood pressure testing. In addition, the company offers telehealth services and prescription delivery services that are thriving as a result of the Covid 19 pandemic and should continue to well once the pandemic is over. The company also plans to open about 1500 HealthHub health centers that will focus mainly on helping those with chronic diseases better manage their illnesses.

CVS Health Corp. has grown its earnings per share (EPS) at an annual rate of 5.1% during its most recent five-year period. The company has achieved an average annual return on equity (ROE) of 11.6% and an average annual return on capital (ROC) of 7.3% during the last five years. The company has a current ratio of 1.0 and a debt-to-equity ratio of 0.97. The company is expected to grow its earnings per share at an annual rate of 4.6% over the long-term. CVS Health Corp. currently pays an annual dividend of 2.62%.

The company was founded in 1949 and is headquartered in Roseland, New Jersey.

Hormel Foods, Corp. #6

NYSE	HRL
Industry	Meat Products
Sector	Consumer Goods
Employees	19,100 (Full Time)
Website	www.hormelfoods.com

Hormel Foods Corp. engages in the production and marketing of a variety of meat and food products in the U.S. and internationally. The company operates through five segments: Grocery Products, Specialty Foods, Refrigerated Foods, Jennie-O Turkey Store, and International & Other. Hormel Foods' products are estimated to be present in more than 81% of U.S. households and are marketed in more than 75 countries. Hormel Foods Corp. was founded in 1891 and is based in Austin, Minnesota.

Hormel Foods Corp. has grown its earnings per share (EPS) at an annual rate of 5.5% during its most recent five-year period. The company has achieved an average annual return on equity (ROE) of 18.2% and an average annual return on capital (ROC) of 16.8% during the last five years. The company has a current ratio of 2.4 and a debt-to-equity ratio of 0.20. The company is expected to grow its earnings per share at an annual rate of 4.1% over the long-term. Hormel Foods Corp. currently pays an annual dividend of 2.21%.

Hormel Foods Corp. was founded in 1891 and is based in Austin, Minnesota.

PepsiCo, Inc. #7

NasdaqGS	PEP
Industry	Beverages, Non-Alcoholic
Sector	Consumer Defensive
Employees	267,000 (Full Time)
Website	www.pepsico.com

PepsiCo, Inc. is a global food and beverage company that manufactures, markets, distributes, and sales a wide-range of foods, beverages, and snacks. The company markets a portfolio of popular brands that include Pepsi-Cola, Quaker, Frito-Lay, Gatorade, and Tropicana. Within the company's portfolio are 23 brands that generate more than $1 billion each in annual sales. PepsiCo, Inc. had net revenue of more than $67 billion in 2019.

PepsiCo, Inc. has grown its earnings per share (EPS) at an annual rate of 4.0% during its most recent five-year period. The company has achieved an average annual return on equity (ROE) of 58.5% and an average annual return on capital (ROC) of 16.8% during the last five years. The company has a current ratio of 0.90 and a debt-to-equity ratio of 3.31. The company is expected to grow its earnings per share at an annual rate of 6.1% over the long-term. PepsiCo, Inc. currently pays an annual dividend of 2.89%.

The company was founded in 1898 and is headquartered in Purchase, New York.

Snap-On, Inc. #8

NYSE	SNA
Industry	Tools & Accessories
Sector	Industrials
Employees	12,800 (Full Time)
Website	www.snapon.com

Snap-on, Inc. is a leading global manufacturer and marketer of tools, equipment, diagnostics, and repair information and systems solutions for professional users worldwide. The company operates through four segments: Snap-On Tools Group, Repair Systems and Information Group, Commercial and Industrial Group, and Financial Services. Snap-On, Inc. has approximately 3,400 franchise vans in the U.S. and approximately 4,700 mobile stores worldwide.

Snap-On, Inc. has grown its earnings per share (EPS) at an annual rate of 11.7% during its most recent five-year period. The company has obtained an average annual return on equity (ROE) of 21.3% and an average annual return on capital (ROC) of 16.4% during the last five years. The company has a current ratio of 2.6 and a debt-to-equity ratio of 0.40. The company is expected to grow its earnings per share at an annual rate of 10.0% over the long-term. Snap-On, Inc. currently pays an annual dividend of 2.87%.

Snap-on, Inc. was founded in 1920 and is headquartered in Kenosha, Wisconsin.

T Rowe Price Group, Inc. #9

Nasdaq GS	TROW
Industry	Asset Management
Sector	Financial
Employees	7,635 (Full Time)
Website	www.trowprice.com

T. Rowe Price Group, Inc. is a global investment management organization. The company offers a broad range of stock, bond, hybrid, and money market funds. It provides its services to individuals, retirement plans, financial intermediaries, institutional investors, and other institutions. The company has more than one trillion dollars in assets under management (AUM). T. Rowe Price Group, Inc. has clients in more than 45 countries worldwide.

T. Rowe Price Group has grown its earnings per share (EPS) at an annual rate of 13.9% during its most recent five-year period. The company has achieved an average annual return on equity (ROE) of 28.2% and an average annual return on capital (ROC) of 27.9% during the last five years. The company has no debt. The company is expected to grow its earnings per share at an annual rate of 12.2% over the long-term. T. Rowe Price Group, Inc. currently pays an annual dividend of 2.32%.

The company was founded in 1937 and is based in Baltimore, Maryland.

Watsco, Inc. #10

NYSE	WSO
Industry	Electronics Wholesale
Sector	Services
Employees	5,800 (Full Time)
Website	www.watsco.com

Watsco, Inc. is the largest distributor of heating, air-conditioning, and refrigeration equipment, and related parts and supplies in the United States. The company serves more than 100,000 dealers and contractors, which serve the Replacement Markets and New Construction Markets. Watsco's focus is on providing replacement equipment and parts. The company has 603 locations in 40 states. The company's annual sales for 2020 were more than $5 billion.

Watsco, Inc. has grown its earnings per share (EPS) at an annual rate of 8.5% during its most recent five-year period. The company has achieved an average annual return on equity (ROE) of 17.8% and an average annual return on capital (ROC) of 14.9% during the last five years. The company has a current ratio of 2.70 and a debt-to-equity ratio of 0.05. Watsco, Inc. is expected to grow its earnings per share at an annual rate of 15.0% over the long-term and currently pays an annual dividend of 2.96%.

Watsco, Inc. was founded in 1945 and is headquartered in Miami, Florida.

Hello Fellow Investor,

Thank you so much for reading *A Beginner's Guide to Dividend Stock Investing*. I hope you enjoyed reading the book as much as I enjoyed researching and writing it. I have certainly enjoyed sharing the knowledge I have obtained through more than a decade of research, study and portfolio management. If you like this book and have a minute to spare, please consider writing a review on the page or website from which you bought the book. Even if you didn't like it, I would appreciate your feedback.

I have provided the link for Amazon below. Thank you so much for reading my book.

In gratitude,

James Pattersenn Jr.

Amazon Link:

https://www.amazon.com/review/create-review/listing

YOUR FREE GIFT

Thanks for purchasing my book!

As a way of showing my appreciation, I want to send you my FREE REPORT.

5 STOCKS THAT WARREN BUFFETT WOULD LOVE

Contained within this report are:

- 5 wonderful companies that Warren Buffett might buy today if given the opportunity.
- The specific criteria for picking Buffett type stocks via value investing.
- Great companies that are practically guaranteed to grow and deliver big returns well beyond the pandemic!

Enter your email at the link below and I will send you a copy of this Free Report:

https://mailchi.mp/b65776af6219/5-stocks-warren-buffett-would-love

Other books by the author

You Can Invest Like A Stock Market Pro:

How to Use Simple and Powerful Strategies of the World's Greatest Investors to Build Wealth

https://www.amazon.com/dp/B07G9PW4F2

Now That You Can Invest Like a Pro:

More Principles and Strategies for Building Wealth Like the World's Greatest Investors

https://www.amazon.com/dp/B07ZJMV7ZK

Common Sense Investing With Stock Screeners

The Intelligent Investor's Guide to Using

Free Online Stock Screeners to Find Winning Stocks

https://www.amazon.com/dp/B08DQM4SQZ

100 Stocks That a Young Warren Buffett Might Buy:

If He Invested Like He Does Today

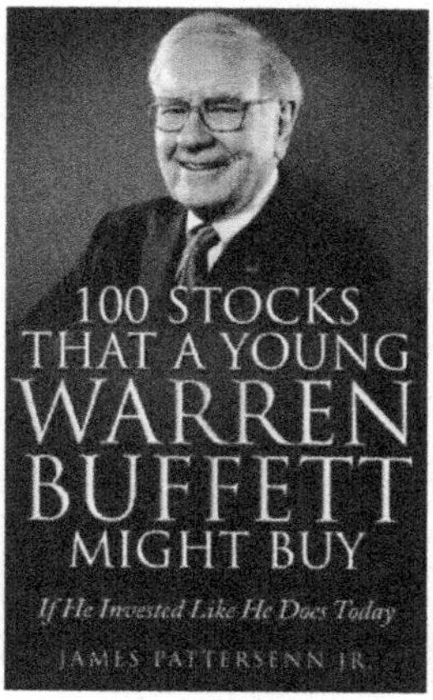

https://www.amazon.com/dp/B07T7XFQNW

Common Sense Investing With Index Funds

How to Build Wealth, Achieve Financial Freedom, and Outperform Most Amateur and Professional Investors Without Really Trying!

https://www.amazon.com/dp/B082V9R886

THE AUTHOR

James Pattersenn Jr. is a self-taught investor and investment researcher that literally spent thousands of hours performing research to determine what does and doesn't work when investing in stocks and the stock market. He has put into practice what he has learned about investing using his own money and says that the investment strategies work, and they work very well.

Pattersenn is a graduate of York Technical College with Honors. He has also extensively studied courses in Business Administration while attending the institution and has earned numerous college credits in the process. He also earned an Undergraduate Certificate in Criminal Justice with Honors from Ashworth College.

Pattersenn served four years in the United States Marine Corps where he was meritoriously promoted twice and received an Honorable Discharge and Good Conduct Award. He was recalled to active duty to serve during Operation Desert Storm and received the National Defense Service Medal as a result.

He enjoys exercising and was a competitive powerlifter many years ago and took first place in the North Carolina State Powerlifting Championship in the 181 pounds class. He now speed walks about every day and practices the martial art known as Hapkido. He was born and resides in the beautiful state of South Carolina with his family.

ACKNOWLEDGMENTS

My sincere thanks to:

Carrie Pattersenn, my sweet and unselfish mother. She taught me the importance of putting the needs of others before my own if I truly wanted to be blessed and to be a blessing.

The great investors who have made this book and all my other books possible because they cared enough to willingly share their wisdom and knowledge about investing with the rest of us.

Angie, a professional graphic designer, whom I found at Fiverr (the world's largest freelance services marketplace). She does amazing work, and you are going to love her prices! If you need an eBook cover or printed book cover, hire her. She can be contacted at https://www.fiverr.com/inbox/pro_ebookcovers

Timason, a professional graphic artist and engineer, whom I discovered at Fiverr. I'm always very happy with the excellent job that he does formatting my books. He does high-quality work at such affordable prices. I will continue to hire him for all of my future projects. He can be found on Fiverr where he has been a member for more than five years with a perfect 5-Star rating! He can be contacted at https://www.fiverr.com/inbox/tlmason

Proof Royalty, a professional proofreading service that does an excellent job of improving my writing to make me look smarter than I really am! Proof Royalty can be contacted at https://www.fiverr.com/inbox/proof_royalty

Most of all, I thank God, the Father, and my Lord Jesus Christ, who is gracious and merciful to all.

Made in the USA
Monee, IL
13 September 2026

62981017R00049